WHY AM I NOT MARRIED?

Soul ties and other mysteries to unlock marital destinies

REV. SHEKINAH E. ATIA

©2019 by Eric Tangumonkem. All rights reserved.

IEM PRESS (PO Box 831001, Richardson, TX 75080) functions only as book publisher. As such, the ultimate design, content, editorial accuracy, and views expressed or implied in this work are those of the author. No part of this publication may be reproduced, stored in a retrieval system, or transmitted in any way by any means—electronic, mechanical, photocopy, recording, or otherwise—without the prior permission of the copyright holder, except as provided by USA copyright law. Unless otherwise noted, all Scriptures are taken from the Holy Bible, New International Version®, NIV®. Copyright © 1973, 1978, 1984, 2011 by Biblica, Inc.™ Used by permission of Zondervan. All rights reserved worldwide. www.zondervan.com

ISBN 10: 1-947662-54-6
ISBN 13: 978-1-947662-54-4

Library of Congress Catalog Card Number: 2019914303

Table of Contents

INTRODUCTION V

PART ONE: THE MYSTERY OF SOUL TIES 1
    THE DEFINITION OF MYSTERY 3
    THE MYSTERY OF SOUL TIES AND THE BATTLE OF
    THE FLESH 7
    THE CONSEQUENCES OF SOUL TIES 19
    GUARDING THE GATES INTO THE SOUL 21
    DELIVERANCE FROM UNGODLY SOUL TIES 23

PART TWO: MYSTERIES TO ENTER YOUR MARITAL DESTINY ... 27
    THE MYSTERY OF LIFE SEASONS AND CREATION 29
    THE MYSTERY OF EXCHANGE 33
    THE MYSTERY OF THE ELDERS AT THE GATES 37
    THE MYSTERY OF VOICES AND DECREES 41
    THE MYSTERY OF THE BLOOD COVENANT 45
    THE MYSTERY OF THE ALTAR AND THE SEED 49

CONCLUSION 51

INTRODUCTION

"And the LORD God said; 'It is not good that the man should be alone; I will make him a helper fit for him'. And out of the ground the LORD God formed every beast of the field and every fowl of the air; and brought them unto Adam to see what he would call them: and whatsoever Adam called every living creature that was the name thereof. And Adam gave names to all cattle, and to the fowl of the air and to every beast of the field; but for Adam there was not found a helper fit for him. And the LORD God caused a deep sleep to fall upon Adam, and he slept: and he took one of his ribs, and closed up the flesh instead thereof; And the rib, which the LORD God had taken from man, made he a woman, and brought her unto the man. And Adam said, this is now bone of my bones, and flesh of my flesh: she shall be called Woman, because she was taken out of Man. Therefore, shall a man leave his father and his mother, and shall cleave unto his wife: and they shall be one flesh. And they were both naked, the man and his wife, and were not ashamed." (Genesis 2:18-25)

Reading the above scripture makes us to understand that God has a particular interest in the institution of marriage, which is a major foundation for family life. Marriage is not an end in itself; yet, it is a very important element in God's restoration agenda especially in these last days. God is a God of family.

> *"For this cause, I bow my knees unto the Father of our Lord Jesus Christ, of whom the whole family in heaven and earth is named"* (Ephesians 3:14-15).

In the past, God used families to fulfill his ambitions for mankind. God has not changed. He is using families in our times and will use families greatly in the finishing of all things. At the end of the day, God will be left with a family. That is, God our Father and all His sons of whom we are will be gathered unto His bosom to live with Him in eternity.

The marriage institution has been under attack and will be under serious attack, especially in these end times. That is why we see all kinds of marital and family perversions like homosexual marriages, which men have invented and do not align with God's Word or divine pattern for marriage. However, God still has a remnant who shall partner with Him in the restoration of the marriage institution and families in this dispensation. Many people desire to get married; yet, very few understand the purpose of marriage. Many people marry for the wrong reasons. You do not marry because you are lonely. Besides, there are many who are married, yet very lonely. You do not marry for sexual intercourse because after the sexual intercourse, what next? You do not marry because you are advanced in age. Marriage is a divine union or covenant to fulfill God's ambition, which entails the mandate God gave man in Genesis 1:28.

The Word of God makes us to understand that it is God's will for His daughters and sons that are ripe for marriage to marry.

INTRODUCTION

"And the LORD God said, 'It is not good that the man should be alone; I will make him a helper fit for him." (Genesis 2:18) "Search from the book of the LORD and read: Not one of these shall fail; not one shall lack her mate. For My mouth has commanded it, and His Spirit has gathered them." (Isaiah 34:16).

Many singles have been waiting upon the Lord, loving Him and serving Him not primarily because they want a life mate. Many people judge themselves, prepared and ready to enter into their marital destinies. To some, marriage proposals are not coming forthcoming. To others, there are marriage proposals that are turned down or when given little consideration, never materialize into a serious relationship. To some, it is always an experience of a serious engagement which ruptures when the families of the concerned are already acquainted with one another till the point of paying the bride price. Many are wondering why these repeated patterns of experiences. Why these delays? The Lord has already provided us with everything that pertains to life and godliness. What then is the problem? Why am I not yet married?

Friends, we are about to explore hidden truths and mysteries that will not only answer that question in the heart of many singles but will help in repositioning them so that they can possess their marital inheritance. These mysteries were revealed to me over the years in the course of my fellowship and walk with the Lord as a single desiring His perfect will for my life in the area of marriage. These mysteries are not only useful to singles but to the married as well. I advise you to be on a fast as you read on. Your destiny is about to experience a major transformation. This is your season and your time is now.

PART ONE

THE MYSTERY OF SOUL TIES

THE DEFINITION OF MYSTERY

> *"And his disciples asked him, saying, what might this parable be? And he said, unto you it is given to know the mysteries of the kingdom of God: but to others in parables; that seeing they might not see and hearing they might not understand." (Luke 8:9-10)*

> *"The secret of the LORD is with them that fear him; and he will shew them his covenant." (Psalms 25:14)*

There is an intimacy married persons cannot share or experience with any third-party except with their legitimate spouses. There is information or secrets that remain between them which no third-party can ever know unless one of them reveals it. Anyone can have access to the Scriptures, but not everyone knows the mysteries of the Kingdom. Mysteries are divine secrets or truths that cannot be revealed just to anyone unless he or she is married to, not just an acquaintance of, His Word. It is reserved to those who have a covenant with Him. Secrets are revealed in the depths of intimacy with the Lord.

> *"O the depth of the riches both of the wisdom and knowledge of God! How unsearchable are his judgments, and his ways past finding out!" (Romans 11:33)*

There are different levels of intimacy or fellowship with the Lord, following the pattern of the tabernacle or temple. There is the first level or outer court level that has natural light, natural wisdom or ability as illumination. This is the initiation level of covenant. This is the gateway to salvation or eternal life. Jesus is the Way, the Truth and the Light. There are three levels of relating with Him. This first level is the Way.

The second level or inner court level (Holy Place) is illuminated by candlesticks, oil and flame. This corresponds to the saved believer that has been filled by the Holy Spirit. At this level, flesh and spirit work together to produce light. This realm of mixture is the realm of the partial or imperfect. It is the level of Truth. You shall know the truth and the truth shall set you free. The truth sanctifies the soul.

The third level is behind the veil. It is the Most Holy Place. God alone is preeminent and initiates every experience at this level. There is no natural light or burning candlesticks. It is all Spirit. There is the unapproachable light of His Presence emanating from between the Cherubim on the Mercy Seat. Jesus is the Light and the manifold Wisdom of God.

> *Mysteries are not for babes. "For everyone that useth milk is unskillful in the word of righteousness: for he is a babe. But strong meat belongeth to them that are of full age, even those who by reason of use have their senses exercised to discern both good and evil." (Hebrews 5:13-14)*

Pray and ask the Lord for the Spirit of wisdom and revelation in the knowledge of Him so that the eyes of your understanding might be enlightened; that ye may know what the hope of his calling is, and the riches of the glory of his inheritance in the saints.

Get ready as we begin this journey of unveiling the mysteries that shall unlock your marital destiny!

THE MYSTERY OF SOUL TIES AND THE BATTLE OF THE FLESH

> *"And it came to pass, when he had made an end of speaking unto Saul that **the soul of Jonathan was knit with the soul of David**, and Jonathan loved him as his own soul. And Saul took him that day and would let him go no more home to his father's house. Then Jonathan and David made a covenant, because he loved him as his own soul. And Jonathan stripped himself of the robe that was upon him, and gave it to David, and his garments, even to his sword, and to his bow, and to his girdle." (1ᵗ Samuel 18:1-4)*

A soul tie is the process by which two or more souls are tied together to become one flesh. It is the cleaving, joining or knitting of souls. This is a mystery. How do you tie two souls together? It is not like taking two cords and tying them together. The knitting of Jonathan's soul to David was a mystery. A covenant was initiated between them by the knitting of their souls. A soul tie is the initiation of covenant. The soul tie between Jonathan and David was a godly or divine soul tie. It is important to establish that not all soul ties are divine.

Godly or Divine Soul Ties

"And the LORD God caused a deep sleep to fall upon Adam, and he slept: and he took one of his ribs, and closed up the flesh instead thereof; And the rib, which the LORD God had taken from man, made he a woman, and brought her unto the man. And Adam said, This is now bone of my bones, and flesh of my flesh: she shall be called Woman, because she was taken out of Man. Therefore, shall a man leave his father and his mother, and shall cleave unto his wife: and they shall be one flesh." (Genesis 2:21-24)

*"And it came to pass, when he had made an end of speaking unto Saul that **the soul of Jonathan was knit with the soul of David**, and Jonathan loved him as his own soul." (1 Samuel 18:1)*

From the above scriptures, we see that these soul ties or covenants were initiated by God to fulfill a righteous purpose. A marriage covenant initiated in a holy and proper context is to serve a divine purpose. That is why marriage is likened to the union of the church (the Bride of Christ) and Christ. It is a mystery. It is through this union that God can manifest His glory.

Although David had a kingly mandate upon his life, he needed not only to know the protocol of the kingly office, but a special kingly impartation to prepare him for his kingly assignment. That is why God initiated a soul tie or covenant between him and Jonathan to accomplish His ambition.

Ungodly Soul Ties

> *"Know ye not that your bodies are the members of Christ? shall I then take the members of Christ, and make them the members of a harlot? God forbid. What? know ye not that he which is joined to a harlot is one body? for two, saith he, shall be one flesh."* (I Corinthians 6:15-16)

There is certain knitting or tying of souls that do not glorify God. Such soul ties or covenants serve the flesh and evil works of darkness; they do not edify its victims nor glorify the Lord.

The Initiation of Soul Ties or Covenants

If a soul tie is the tying or marrying of souls together, then the question we have to answer to is "How is this covenant or marriage of souls together contracted?"

1. Sexual activities

Whether you call it sexual intercourse or outer course, there is always a transfer that takes place when persons involve themselves in sexual activities. The Scripture says that he who is joined to a harlot is one body with her. Even if the joining is not with a harlot, so long as there is closeness through sexual intercourse or other sexual activities, a soul tie is initiated. There is a transfer that takes place in that process when a man or a woman projects himself or herself in a sexual act. When a man projects himself in sexual intercourse, he releases strength, his life or a seed. Women, on the other hand, receive the seed or a deposit of his strength or life. With the evil sexual perversion we see around us, like homosexual practices, we can establish the fact that soul ties through sexual activities are not only amongst persons of the same sex. They can be contracted through homosexual activities, too.

Many people call themselves single because they are not legally joined in holy matrimony to their God-ordained mates. But the Lord made me to understand that although these singles are not married in the literal sense, a lot of them are NOT single! They are not single at the soul level. They are still bound by unbroken covenants or soul ties. Soul ties or covenants that were initiated while they were not yet born again and even after they became born again. Every time you had sexual intercourse or outer course with someone, a marriage or covenant was contracted. Your soul was tied to his or hers. He or she became your soul mate. You see a beautiful single sister or handsome single brother in the Lord who has contracted several covenants or marriages yet trusting the Lord for his or her ordained mate.

Not only singles are victims of soul ties through sexual activities. Even some married persons are bound by soul ties. Some bring it along into their marital homes while others contract it through the act of fornication while in their marital homes.

2. Supernatural means

We see that the soul tie between David and Jonathan was not through sexual intercourse. It was not only through a supernatural means, but it was divine. We must understand that there are different realms which manifestations can take place. The lowest realm is the natural realm. After the natural realm is the supernatural realm. The highest realm is the divine realm. Satan operates in the natural and supernatural realms. He was cast to the earth after his rebellion against

God. He is the prince of the air. He operates a lot of counterfeit manifestations in the natural and supernatural realm.

> "But while men slept, his enemy came and sowed tares among the wheat and went his way." (Matthew 13:25)

Some soul ties or covenants were contracted through supernatural means, especially during night seasons when men are asleep and less active physically. Sometimes. it is during the day while you are taking a nap. The initiation takes place in the realm of your soul especially through dreams. You have persons who testify of having made love to unknown or known persons in their dreams. You get up in the morning with a sexual discharge. Many say they are virgins in the physical sense; yet spiritually, they are not because of such supernatural happenings. I remember dating a man in the days of my ignorance and he called me on phone one morning to tell me how he made love to me throughout the night and it was quite good. If that is not a mystical or supernatural happening, how can you explain such a mystery? I slept in my house and did not even dream about him in the night. How come he made love to me throughout the night if it was not through supernatural means? In as much as our dream realm can be a gateway for evil works by unclean spirits, it does not mean it cannot be a gateway for good works, too. Some people have experienced divine impartations and angelic visitations through dreams.

Apart from sexual intercourse or the laying on of hands through which certain transfers can be done, there are other means by which soul covenants can be initiated supernaturally. There are persons who do incisions, commonly known as "blood pacts". They use blades, knives or sharp objects to incise themselves until there is the flow of blood. They mix up the blood, lick it and declare vows over themselves that binds their souls together.

3. Other physical or spiritual articles

A lot of soul ties have been initiated indirectly through physical items or articles such as food, clothes, perfumes, money, jewelries, etc.

> "For my flesh is meat indeed, and my blood is drink indeed. He that eateth my flesh, and drinketh my blood, dwelleth in me, and I in him." (John 6:55-56)

From the above scripture, Jesus presents a meal that brings about a soul tie with Him when we eat it. Not every physical or spiritual food is good for your consumption. You are what you eat. When certain things are added in food or certain declarations made over the food before it is consumed, there are sure consequences. That is why you have persons who visit witch doctors that instruct them to carry out certain prophetic actions like washing of their sexual organs with water and dropping some of the water in the food before giving to the person they desire to render their captive. We see a responsible married man who, after eating in his mistress' house, becomes obsessed with her up to the point of neglecting his family. Many are victims of soul ties through food. Watch your eating habits. Do not just eat everything that is given to you. Some people get initiated into a covenant through the spiritual food they eat in their dreams. That is why you must pray after such experiences and seal your prayer with the Holy Communion meal.

Some physical or spiritual gifts you receive from people are points of contact to bind or enslave your soul. There are young women or men who are very materialistic. You are in Christendom, yet you lust passionately after worldly things. You want to by all possible means meet up with the latest fashion. You do not care if you have to hook up with another person's spouse in the world or in Christendom. You see a brother coveting the riches of a well-to-do single sister. The reason why they prepare gifts and give them to you is to bind you to them. Young girl, how can you be so naïve and blind? Some of those jewelries, perfumes, clothes and money given to you are intended to bind your soul to his. Besides, what should you be doing with some other person's spouse? A second-hand commodity! You are far above that foolishness. Psalm 49:20 says, "Man that is in honor, and understandeth not, is like the beasts that perish." Single person, you are honorable and precious in the sight of God, your father. He esteems you higher than you have placed yourself in want of acceptance and marriage. Therefore, deliver yourself! Not every gift is a good gift. What is the purpose of the gift? What is the motive of the giver? You need to be sensitive and discern with spiritual insight the kinds of gifts that are offered to you as well as the heart of the giver. Do not accept every gift from people, no matter how nice they might appear before you. Some people receive gifts in their dreams. Some young girls have contracted marriages in their dreams through the wedding ring that was worn on their finger. When such thing happens, do not treat it lightly. Reject the ring and break the bond by using the anointing oil to anoint your finger.

4. Communication

"It is the spirit that quickeneth; the flesh profiteth nothing: the words that I speak unto you, they are spirit, and they are life." (John 6:63)

Some soul ties or covenants have been initiated through consistent communication through books, telephone, Internet, video, and direct verbal communications. Words have spiritual impact. The power of life and death lies in the tongue. Words are used to program your soul. That is why if you have related emotionally with someone for a long period of time, he/she has such a strong influence on you even when the relationship is ruptured. Women are influenced by what they hear, while men are moved by what they see. With all kinds of technological devices nowadays, communication is very easy. Young people spend hours on telephone calls or Internet chats. The phenomenon nowadays is Internet spouses. You see young beautiful girls exposing their bodies through videos or photographs to win the love of an old, retired, cranky, funny-looking man who is old enough to be their grandfather for want of money and other "good things" in life. The same is with young men who hook up with grandmas as their wives. A lot of young folks indulge in watching pornographic films. A major device via which the kingdom of darkness shall operate in these end times is through the media. Most music and film industries are mediums to communicate unclean spirits. All kinds of immoral slimes are released through the television. Do not feed your eyes and ears with all kinds of junk. Let your conversations be savored or seasoned with grace. Do not just read any kind of books or magazines. Many satanic cults or sects use books to initiate men. You must make a careful choice of the writers to which you submit yourself.

The Battle of the Soul

> *"He hath delivered my soul in peace from the battle that was against me: for there were many with me." (Psalm 55:18)*

> *"For what shall it profit a man, if he shall gain the whole world, and lose his own soul?" (Mark 8:36)*

> *"Beloved, I wish above all things that thou mayest prosper and be in health, even as thy soul prospereth." (3 John 2)*

The soul is an intermediary between your spirit and your body. It is a major interest for God as well as Satan. The spiritual battle is essentially for the souls of men. Many became victims of soul ties or covenants because they did not have an understanding of the spiritual warfare at their soul level. Whatever or whosoever is in possession of your soul possesses or controls your destiny. The state of your soul will determine the prosperity of the different areas of your life. That is why it is very important to renew your mind with the Word of God and to guard your heart diligently since it is the source of the issues of life. The Bible says, "If any man be in Christ, he is a new creature; old things are past and all things have become new." How come we are still bound by soul ties after our conversion? When you become born again, you receive a new spirit from the Lord. However, your soul needs to be continually purged from your old man of sin and all the junk it received in the past as you continue to follow the Lord.

> *"If so be that ye have heard him, and have been taught by him, as the truth is in Jesus: That ye put off concerning the former conversation the old man, which is corrupt according to the deceitful lusts; And be renewed in the spirit of your mind; And that ye put on the new man, which after God is created in righteousness and true holiness." (Ephesians 4:21-24)*

The purging of the soul comes through a daily self-denial and death to the flesh and all its lusts. The old man must be put away and the new man put on. This is known as sanctification. This process of sanctification is not a religious two-day or seven-day fast. Apostle Paul in Galatians 2:20 called it a daily death to the flesh. It is a consistent crucifixion of the old man and his deeds. It is denial to the tempting lusts of your flesh. It is a consistent renewal of your mind by the Word of God (Romans 12:1-2). It is the yielding over of your will and emotions to the will of God. This is our greatest warfare. It is not easy to deny yourself its desires. Every day, it is a major battle because we find ourselves in the midst of evil and corrupt systems. We are in this world yet not of the world. You go about your daily activities and there are temptations that you would face. As a beautiful young girl or woman, men will be attracted to you. You know the kind of men that move you. Besides, your eyes were not made for decoration. Sometimes, you see yourself lusting after a handsome man. You fantasize and wish he could cuddle you in his arms. There are such periods especially during your ovulation season whereby your sexual appetite is difficult to tame. You just feel like having some good sex. The same is with some pious brothers who make up their minds to live a pure life. Out there, you encounter some good-looking well-figured creature with beautiful curved buttocks and apple breasts. Heat rushes through your veins. You do not want to look, but your eyes somehow enjoy the beauty it is beholding at that time. You know the kind of woman that moves you. At times, the battle will be at home where no one is watching you. You have been starved from sexual intercourse for a long time. You zap through the channels and fall on the channel showing some pornography. You watch a little and are trapped by the cries of the sexual scene. Finally, you go to bed and masturbate yourself to orgasm. There are occasions you just desire to have it all night long with the opposite sex. If the battle is not related to sex, it could be a date proposal by some uncircumcised son or daughter of the Philistines. Sometimes, it is the spouse of some other person. He offers you huge sums of money. He proposes to open you a bank account. He gives you all kinds of material gifts. Your flesh says a loud YES while the spirit man uses the word in you to raise a standard against that temptation.

Two laws are fighting within you to enforce themselves. One of the laws is the law of sin and death, while the other law is the law of the Spirit of life in Christ Jesus. You cannot serve two masters. You can obey only one at a time (Romans 6-8). At this time, you need to cry to the Holy Spirit for help; otherwise, you will fall into that temptation which shall eventually corrupt your soul. This is how the devil has many bound at the level of their emotions, minds and will. It is only by renewing your mind in the Word and walking in the spirit that you would be able to tame the lusts of the flesh. You shall always face diverse battles as long as you live on the earth, but if you yield yourself to the Lord, you shall always be victorious.

THE CONSEQUENCES OF SOUL TIES

Soul ties or covenants affect us in diverse ways. The soul tie between David and Jonathan brought about a kingly impartation or transfer from the life of Jonathan unto David. Many are carriers of the virtues or destinies of others via soul ties. The bloodline patterns of an individual become your experience as a result of a soul tie. Some of our lives are upside down because of soul ties. Unusual unfavorable occurrences become our story due to such soul exchanges or transfer. Some deadly diseases are contracted via soul ties.

> "He that diggeth a pit shall fall into it; and whoso breaketh an hedge, a serpent shall bite him."
> (Ecclesiastes 10:8)

Soul ties break the hedge or walls of your soul. A battered or damaged soul is open to the activities of unclean spirits. It becomes a favorable environment for demonic attacks.

In some cases, soul ties result in feelings of guilt, sorrow, regret, and condemnation especially if it is related to sexual or emotional relationships. It promotes certain habits like sexual promiscuity and covetousness. These issues consequently affect your fellowship with the Lord.

Soul ties result in relational difficulties and incompatibility. That is why the rate of divorce is rampant. Most often, quarrels and disputes amongst couples, as well as infidelity in marriage are as a result of the activities of spirit husbands or wives that came through soul ties. An ungodly soul tie in the case of married individuals brings about consistent competition of that illegal soul mate with your legitimate spouse. You want him to act or treat you like your ex-soul mate in sexual, financial and social issues. For singles, it negatively influences their choice of a life mate for marriage. You unconsciously or consciously choose based on the qualities of some of your ex-soul mates. Most broken marriage engagements or cases of celibacy are as a result of soul ties. That is why you need a purification of wrong paradigms, thoughts patterns and systems in your mind. You need to reprogram your mind in God's Word in the area of marriage.

Other consequences of soul ties are the strange repeated incidences or cycles in different life seasons. Most young girls or women will tell you that they experience sexual encounters with ex-soul mates during their ovulation period. For others, it is repeated broken marriage engagements, especially during special marriage seasons or specific periods of the year. For married women, it is repeated miscarriages; in some cases, barrenness.

GUARDING THE GATES INTO THE SOUL

Some major gateways or doors of entry into your soul are the ears, the eyes, the tongue or mouth, and sex organs (Genesis 3:1-7). You must watch your communication habits. Shut the doors of communication to your past life and experiences that keep your soul entangled in unhealthy experiences. Delete telephone numbers and email contacts of those old friends or any of your present acquaintances that have an ungodly influence upon your life. Be careful of the things you watch on TV. Watch out for the kinds of confessions you make. Tie your mind with God's word by meditating upon it day and night. Speak out loud God's word over your life, especially when you sense immoral thought patterns, imaginations or presence creeping into your mind.

DELIVERANCE FROM UNGODLY SOUL TIES

"Bring my soul out of prison, that I may praise thy name: the righteous shall compass me about; for thou shalt deal bountifully with me." (Psalm 142:7)

One of the reasons why your God-ordained mate cannot be joined to you is because you are NOT single. You are entangled with a soul mate. There is no room for your God-ordained mate because there is an illegal occupant in his/her place. You need to be purged from soul ties to become single in your heart with the Lord and to make room for your God-ordained mate.

The reason why this enemy of your soul has been exposed is to alert you that it is time to execute God's judgment upon it no matter how long it has been oppressing you. Your deliverance is ripe. The time of your liberation is now.

Prayer Points

- I acknowledge I have sinned against you, Lord. I repent of every sin in my life especially sexual sins manifested through my thoughts or actions in Jesus' name (1 John 1:6-9, Hebrews 13:4).

- Call by name everyone you had any sexual or emotional entanglement with before. Summon their spirit to your prayer altar and renounce every covenant you had with him or her. For example, Gabriel, I summon your spirit to this altar and I renounce and break every ungodly covenant I had with you in Jesus' name. I divorce you, in Jesus' name. You are not my husband, in Jesus' name.

- By the Word of God (Hebrews 4:12), let every ungodly soul tie in my life be subjected to God's judgment, in Jesus' name.

- Holy Spirit of God, overshadow me and by Your anointing, let every ungodly yoke and tie in my soul be broken, in Jesus' name (Isaiah 10:27). (Anoint yourself with oil.)

- Lord Holy Spirit, do a surgical operation in my soul and remove every illegal occupant in the space the mate You have prepared for me is supposed to occupy, in Jesus' name (Isaiah 34:15-16). Father, uproot every evil planting in my marital destiny, in the name of Jesus (Matthew 15:13).

- Eat a pinch of salt and decree a divine cleansing and healing of your entire system from every deposit that is in you that is not divine, in Jesus' name (2 Kings 2:19-22).

- By the Word of God, shut every gateway that gives access to any illegal spirit or soul husband or wife in your life, especially through your dreams in the night seasons (Isaiah 22:22).

- In the name of Jesus, bind and cast out the stronghold of sexual immorality programmed against your marital destiny (Mark 3:27). Acknowledge and declare in Jesus' name the Holy Ghost as the stronghold of your body, which is God's temple (Luke 11:21)

- Renew your covenant with the Lord Jesus. Ask the Holy Spirit to knit your soul with His, in Jesus' name (2 Corinthians 5:17).
- Decree total restoration of everything that was wasted or robbed from your life as a result of sexual sin or the evil activities of illegal spirit or soul mates (Joel 2:25-27, Hosea 6:1-2).

Finally, I will advise you to sort out any physical articles that were given to you by ex-soul mates and give them away. As long as they are still in your possession, they will act as points of contact that will remind you of past experiences. I personally cleaned my home of gifts and things that were given to me by ex-soul mates. Do not keep their photographs with you anymore. Destroy them.

> *"For everyone shall be salted with fire, and every sacrifice shall be salted with salt." (Mark 9:49). "And there are three that bear witness in earth, the Spirit, and the water, and the blood: and these three agree in one." (1 John 5:8)*

Use the blood of Jesus and covenant your sexual organs to the Lord. Add salt in water and bath yourself prophetically for three days. For young girls or women who experience sex with soul mates during their ovulation period, I will advise you to master your menstrual cycle, take Holy Communion during such periods and wage war in prayers during midnight hours.

It is one thing to be delivered and yet another thing to remain delivered. Pray that the Lord will bring new beginnings and new relationships into your life that will edify you and glorify God. Continue to renew and bind your mind with the Word of God daily. Guard the gateways into your soul diligently. Continue to yield to the Holy Spirit.

If soul tie is not a factor in why you are not married, then position yourself in the mysteries and prayers in the second part of this book as you prepare for the fulfillment of your marital destiny.

PART TWO

MYSTERIES TO ENTER YOUR MARITAL DESTINY

THE MYSTERY OF LIFE SEASONS AND CREATION

"To everything there is a season, and a time to every purpose under the heaven:" (Ecclesiastes 3:1)

"And of the children of Issachar, which were men that had understanding of the times, to know what Israel ought to do:" (1 Chronicle 12:32)

"And God said, 'Let there be lights in the firmament of the heaven to divide the day from the night; and let them be for signs, and for seasons, and for days, and years.'" (Genesis 1:14)

A lot of people are so ignorant about the mysteries of seasons and times and the role of creation in the fulfillment of God's ambition in their lives. The Lord has brought to us at different times our marital inheritance, but because of lack of understanding and wisdom, we missed it. How do you know your season of marriage is ripe? Your Father God will reveal it to you. Another sign is marriage proposal or proposals. You suddenly become very visible to those who are familiar and live in the same environment with you. Sometimes, word of prophecies will come to confirm what the Lord has already spoken to you. Marriage is not a wedding. A lot of singles prepare for a wedding ceremony rather than for a married life.

There is a SEASON of PREPARATION and a TIME of MANIFESTATION. Some of our seasons were manipulated by strange happenings. Sometimes, the spirit of wickedness through men attacked our marital destinies, as was the case of the children of Israel and the Amalekites in Judges 6:1-6. If you look closely at Psalm 24:1 and Revelation 12:1-16, you will understand that creation should be engaged in the fulfillment of your marital destiny when your season is ripe for marriage. How then do you engage creation in the battle of your marital destiny?

Prayer Points

- Subject to God's throne all evil manipulations, works of witchcrafts, satanic altars and foundations, demonic programming, divinations by any evil man, woman, or spirit in the underworld, on the earth, in the waters, and in the heavens that seek to monitor, thwart the purposes of God and rob you during your life seasons, especially during your menstrual cycle or harvest seasons (Numbers 23:23).
- Earth, earth, oh earth, open up your mouth and vomit out anything related to my marital destiny that has been buried in you, in Jesus' name. I command the fire of God to consume every altar that has been built upon you that is working against my marital destiny, in Jesus' name.
- Oh belly of the waters, vomit out anything related to my marital destiny that has been buried in you, in Jesus' name.
- I command the constellations to fight my course against every wickedness that has been programmed in them

against my marital destiny, in Jesus' name (Isaiah 13:10-11, Joshua 10:13).

- I command creation to operate circumstances that will relocate my life mate to me in this season, in Jesus' name.

- I decree favorable divine happenings that will cause our paths to cross in this season, in Jesus' name.

- I release the fire of judgment against every power seeking to suppress and destroy my marital harvest in this season, in Jesus' name (Judges 6:1-6).

- I call upon the angels in charge of my marital destiny to swiftly execute the Word of God concerning my marital destiny, in Jesus' name. May they transport and bring to me my life mate in this season, in Jesus' name.

- I command creation to release every resource I need to fulfill my marital destiny in this season, in Jesus' name.

THE MYSTERY OF EXCHANGE

"Then came there two women, that were harlots, unto the king, and stood before him. And the one woman said, O my lord, I and this woman dwell in one house; and I was delivered of a child with her in the house. And it came to pass the third day after that I was delivered, that this woman was delivered also: and we were together; there was no stranger with us in the house, save we two in the house. And this woman's child died in the night; because she overlaid it. And she arose at midnight, and took my son from beside me, while thine handmaid slept, and laid it in her bosom, and laid her dead child in my bosom. And when I rose in the morning to give my child suck, behold, it was dead: but when I had considered it in the morning, behold, it was not my son, which I did bear." (1 Kings 3:16-22)

Marital destinies can be exchanged. This is what I call the mystery of exchange. The enemy desires us to accept deformed and ugly marital destinies, which have the form of godliness, yet it is not divine. Some time ago after praying seriously about my marital destiny, the Lord through a dream revealed to me how my wedding feast was already ready, with the guests sitting in church waiting for me to come in. I was hesitant to go in because my wedding gown was old-fashioned and unusually big on me. The same was with my shoes. The worst was my hairdo. I was putting on an old-fashioned hair wig instead of having a stylish hairdo. I finally refused to enter the church and I woke up from my sleep. When I sought the Lord concerning that dream, He made me understand that my attire was exchanged with that of another person. At that same period, I had this marriage proposal which had a form of godliness; yet, it was very questionable. The Lord told me if I accept that proposal, I will be entering into an inconvenienced marriage life. Satan might tempt you to believe age is against you, family and friends may mock at you and push you to accept any choice that comes your way. Watch out! Go back to God to reveal to you the original image of your marital destiny and refuse to succumb to any worldly proposal or standard.

Prayer Points

- I command a restitution of every satanic exchange of my marital destiny in the realm of the spirit and the marine world, especially in the night seasons, in the name of Jesus.

- I command my rightful marital destiny to be restored to me in Jesus' name.

- I denounce and reject any counterfeit husband/wife, in the name of Jesus.

- I denounce and reject every marriage gown/attire and crown that is not mine, in Jesus' name. I command a release of my rightful complete marriage attire, in Jesus' name.

- I dethrone every illegal occupant in my marital destiny, in Jesus' name (Isaiah 47:1-2).
- Lord, make room for me in the arena of marriage, in Jesus' name (Psalm 118).
- I commit my spirit, soul and body to the Holy Spirit. By the help of the Holy Spirit, I make room in my heart for God's ordained mate for my life, in Jesus' name.
- I reject every idiosyncrasy, thought pattern and system that want to influence me negatively to exchange my divine marital destiny, in Jesus' name.

THE MYSTERY OF THE ELDERS AT THE GATES

Then went Boaz up to the gate, and sat him down there: and, behold, the kinsman of whom Boaz spake came by; unto whom he said, 'Ho, such a one! turn aside, sit down here.' And he turned aside and sat down. And he took ten men of the elders of the city, and said, Sit ye down here. And they sat down. And he said unto the kinsman, Naomi, that is come again out of the country of Moab, selleth a parcel of land, which was our brother Elimelech's: And I thought to advertise thee, saying, Buy it before the inhabitants, and before the elders of my people. If thou wilt redeem it, redeem it: but if thou wilt not redeem it, then tell me, that I may know: for there is none to redeem it beside thee; and I am after thee. And he said, I will redeem it. Then said Boaz, 'What day thou buyest the field of the hand of Naomi, thou must buy it also of Ruth the Moabitess, the wife of the dead, to raise up the name of the dead upon his inheritance.' (Ruth 4:1-5)

And it came to pass, that in the morning, behold, it was Leah: and he said to Laban, 'What is this thou hast done unto me? Did not I serve with thee for Rachel?

> *Wherefore then hast thou beguiled me?' And Laban said, 'It must not be so done in our country, to give the younger before the firstborn. Fulfill her week, and we will give thee this also for the service which thou shalt serve with me yet seven other years.' And Jacob did so and fulfilled her week: and he gave him Rachel, his daughter, to wife also. (Genesis 29:25-28)*

Elders at the gates of your marital destiny have the power to influence it negatively or positively. Elders at the gates are those who have power to influence your marital destinies through their decisions or counsels. Reading from above, Laban and Boaz were elders at the gates. Boaz influenced Ruth's marital destiny positively, while Laban delayed Rachel's marital destiny. Many times, these elders those you submit to, for example, your biological parents, family relatives, spiritual leaders, and your friends (especially brethren in the faith). I had treated cases of broken engagements just because of tribal differences. Some elders at the gates of your marital destiny will delay your destiny because the brother is from a tribe like Bassa. They have a bad testimony about Bassa people. Some will stick to the fact that the testimony of the sister's past life was not good; consequently, she should not be accepted into their family. Many beautiful engagements are ruptured because of such cultural, family values and doctrinal differences.

Prayer Points

- In the name of Jesus, I pronounce judgment upon the enemies at the gates of my marital destiny (Genesis 22:17).
- I command the gates and doors of my marital destiny to be lifted up such that the will of my Father concerning

my marital destiny should be fulfilled in this season, in Jesus' name (Psalm 24:7-10).

- May every elder at the gate (those who have power of decision or influence over my marital destiny) and who seeks to manipulate the wrong person in my rightful place be confounded, in Jesus' name (Genesis 29:26, Ruth 4:1-3).

- No power shall thwart God's purposes for my marital destiny, in Jesus' name (Job 42:2).

- Let there be no wisdom, counsel or knowledge against God's will concerning my marital destiny in this season, in Jesus' name (Proverbs 21:30).

- Let all men be liars and let God be true. Let His word prevail concerning my marital destiny, in Jesus' name.

- Earth, you belong to the Lord. All peoples in you belong to the Lord. The hearts of kings belong to You, Lord and You direct them wherever you please. Give no peace to any man standing against my marital destiny, in Jesus' name! Oh earth and constellations, trouble them with sleeplessness until they abide to God's will concerning my marital destiny, in Jesus' name.

- Father, accord me favor before all those who have any form of influence over my marital destiny, in Jesus' name.

THE MYSTERY OF VOICES AND DECREES

"A man's belly shall be satisfied with the fruit of his mouth; and with the increase of his lips shall he be filled. Death and life are in the power of the tongue: and they that love it shall eat the fruit thereof." (Proverbs 18:20-21)

"There are, it may be, so many kinds of voices in the world, and none of them is without signification." (1 Corinthians 14:10)

Many people have treated lightly the issue of spoken words or declarations in the area of their marital destiny. Sometime back, there was this divorced man who was interested in marrying me. I never had peace about the relationship. During our encounters, he will say things like, "You are my soul mate. You are my wife. You shall bear my children." At first, I ignored it. Later, the Lord revealed to me that he was indirectly programming my marital destiny through his words. And I needed to reject and make declarations to counteract it. Words have creative power. Words can build or destroy destinies. Don't ignore it when someone says to you that no one shall marry you. Even if it was just a joke, quickly correct it and declare that you will not only marry, but you shall marry a wonderful man or woman.

Prayer Points

- Woe unto them that decree unrighteous decrees and that write grievousness which they have prescribed against my marital destiny, in Jesus' name!
- By the blood of Jesus, I silence every prophetic utterances or voices that had spoken or is still speaking contrary to the will of God concerning my marital destiny, in Jesus' name.
- Heavenly Father, thunder over the voices speaking evil against my marital destiny in the heavens, the earth and the marine world, in Jesus' name (Psalm 29).
- May every satanic decree from any altar or evil foundation working against my marital destiny catch fire, in Jesus' name.
- I decree judgment over the powers of darkness that have resisted the deliverance of my marital destiny, in Jesus' name. May the angel of death kill whatever represents the source of your strength, in Jesus' name.
- I decree miscarrying wombs to every conspiracy against the fulfillment of my marital destiny in this season, in Jesus' name.
- I decree I shall marry, in Jesus' name. I decree my marriage shall no longer be delayed, in Jesus' name. I decree that divine marriage is my inheritance in Christ Jesus.
- By the voice of God's word, I call out my God-ordained mate to wake up from any deep sleep he/she is in, in Jesus' name (Genesis 2:21, Daniel 8:18, Daniel 10:9, John 11:43-44, John 5:28).

- I prophesy life into my marital destiny, in Jesus' name. I decree a resurrection of my marital destiny, in Jesus' name. I command the wind from the Lord's presence to revive my marital destiny, in Jesus' name. I command the joining of the broken and lost bones of my marital destiny, in Jesus' name. Let there be sinews, flesh and skin on the bones, in Jesus' name. (Ezekiel 37:1-8)

THE MYSTERY OF THE BLOOD COVENANT

"But now hath he obtained a more excellent ministry, by how much also he is the mediator of a better covenant, which was established upon better promises. For if that first covenant had been faultless, then should no place have been sought for the second." (Hebrews 8:6-7)

"And to Jesus the mediator of the new covenant, and to the blood of sprinkling, that speaketh better things than that of Abel." (Hebrews 12:24)

A covenant is a formal sealed agreement or contract between two or more persons. The conditions of the covenant, if well kept, will bless you. If not respected, it will act as a curse to you. God is a God of covenant and He functions by covenant. Our covenant with Him is higher than any other covenant we might have contracted in the past. God's covenant with us was initiated via our father Abraham and it was a very special covenant. He made provisions in the covenant to always back us even when we do not keep all the conditions. This is not, however, a passport to sin. The wages of sin is death. The good news about our covenant with God is that it is able to deliver us from any other covenant that was negatively binding our marital destinies. Some singles are still bound unconsciously to marriage proposals or engagements that never materialized. A higher covenant breaks a lesser one. If the blood of animals could deliver the whole nation of Israel from 430 years of affliction and oppression, dear friend, cheer up because the blood of Jesus can do far better in your favor.

Prayer Points

- By the blood of Jesus, I cancel every handwritten ordinance against my marital destiny.
- By the sprinkling of the blood of Jesus, I silence every tongue and thoughts patterns in my past life speaking contrary to God's will for me in marriage. I sanctify my hearing with the blood of Jesus.
- By the blood of Jesus, I wipe out every satanic name on my fore face working against my marital destiny.
- By the blood of Jesus, I anoint myself against every repelling presence or stigma (especially tribal stigmas) upon my life that hinders my divine mate to be joined to me. The blood of Jesus from this day gives me a sweet smell and presence.
- By the blood of Jesus, I judge every family blood line pattern working against my marital destiny.
- I sprinkle the blood of Jesus over my dream realm.
- Let the blood of Jesus judge and destroy every satanic vision and dream released from the pit of hell against my marital destiny.
- By the blood of Jesus, I access the wisdom, knowledge, understanding and other divine resources necessary to prepare me for the fulfillment of my marital destiny.

- Prophetically, use the blood of Jesus and wash your sexual organs praying against ungodly covenants that were initiated via sexual intercourse. Seal that gateway with the blood of Jesus against any spirit husband or wife.

THE MYSTERY OF THE ALTAR AND THE SEED

An altar is a gateway into the spiritual world. He who owns an altar governs the land or domain where the altar is found. An altar is a platform for spiritual exchange or transfer between a higher and a lower power. The cross was God's altar through which the plague of satanic oppression upon humanity was crushed. An altar without a seed is impotent. What empowers your altar is the seed you place on it. What empowered God's altar was His seed (His only begotten son Jesus). Like David, you need to connect to an altar and place a sacrificial seed to put an end to your marital dilemma (1 Chronicles 21). The seed goes to the priest who ministers faithfully to that altar and who can call on God on your behalf. The priest shall receive your seed and release the blessing upon your life.

A priest is an intermediary between a deity and man. Some priests serve evil purposes while others serve divine purposes. Your seed is the guarantee of your future harvest. Your seed will open doors for you. It will wage battle for you until you enter into the fulfillment of your marital destiny. You can as well build a personal prayer altar to give God a platform to continue to address issues affecting your marital destiny.

Prayer Points

- Pray against any ungodly altar(s) and foundations raised on your behalf anywhere that is working against your marital destiny, in Jesus' name. Command the fire of God to consume them, in Jesus' name.

- Declare God's judgment against any satanic priest manipulating your marital destiny, in Jesus' name.

- Present a prophetic seed to the Lord and commission it to wage war in the favor of your marital destiny. Ask the Lord to lead you to a fertile ground (the appropriate person, that is, a servant of God) where you can sow your seed and declare a word of blessing over you.

CONCLUSION

The table of the Lord or Holy Communion: Break bread by renewing your covenant vows with the Lord using Hosea 2:16-23. Pledge your virginity, the purity of your heart and soul to the Lord. Desire only the perfect will of the Father concerning your marital destiny. Like the daughters of Zelophehad (Numbers 27:1-7, Numbers 36:6), lay claim to your marital inheritance, in Jesus' name. Above all, continue to abide in worship and meditate upon His word day and night while you remain focused in doing your divine assignment.

You were not born for marriage. Your life purpose is greater than any marriage you can get into. Marriage is not an end, but a means to an End. Marriage is not a wedding. Marriage is not a means of escape from sexual temptations. Marriage is not sex. Marriage is a ministry. Continue to prepare and equip yourself for that ministry (ministering firstly to the Lord, then to your spouse, your children and lastly, those that are connected to your destiny). Prepare to become an asset and not a liability to your God-ordained mate, family and generation. Work on your character or attitude.

Ask the Lord to help and guide you in choosing your life mate when the opportunity presents itself. Let your choice be based not only on temporal factors (job status, physical qualities, age, educational status, etc.). Man looks at the outward appearance, but God sees the heart. You need divine insight, foresight, godly counsel and God's mercy to help you choose someone who can accommodate you to where God has destined for you.

You are not married until you are married! I encourage you to persist in these prayers until you enter your marital destiny. You are blessed for life. This is your season and your time is NOW!

Shalom!
Rev. Shekinah.Atia

To order additional copies of this book call:

317-975-0806

Or visit our website at

www.iempublishing.com

If you enjoyed this quality custom-published book

Drop by our website for more books and information

"Inspiring, equipping, and motivating one author at a time."

www.ingramcontent.com/pod-product-compliance
Lightning Source LLC
Chambersburg PA
CBHW031639160426
43196CB00006B/479